SPEAKING OUT : VOICES OF ADULT CHILDREN OF DIVORCE

A RESOURCE GUIDE FOR FAMILIES IN ANY STAGE OF DIVORCE

JODY COMINS, MSW

A BETTER WAY PUBLISHING

CONTENTS

Preface	vii
Introduction	xiii
1. Mediation Works When You Take the Time to Nurture Your Divorce	1
2. Telling Your Children	5
3. Most Difficult Situation Being a Child of Divorce	10
4. How did it feel to Have Divorced Parents?	15
5. Divided Loyalty	19
6. Caught in the Middle	23
7. Navigating the Holidays in a Divorced Family	27
8. "Parentification"	29
9. How Custody Arrangements Evolved Over Time	33
10. Think of it Like a Business Relationship	38
11. Advice from the Experts	40
12. More Advice From the Experts	45
13. Positive Outcomes of Divorce as Felt by Adult Children of Divorce	50
14. Positive Outcomes of Divorce - Part Two	54
Conclusion	59
Acknowledgments	61
About the Author	63

Dedicated to my older brother, Michael Comins, and my younger sister, Jami Comins Schultz, for traveling on this journey with me. Only my siblings can understand exactly who I am and how I operate because of our shared childhood.

PREFACE

You probably didn't stand under the wedding canopy and plan on getting divorced, but here you are.

Society is full of negative expressions for divorced couples and families- "he's from a broken home," "their marriage failed", etc., but it doesn't have to be a negative. If you work as hard planning your divorce as you did planning your wedding, being divorced can simply be the next great chapter in your life.

The idea for this book started at a friend's house, when my husband and I were talking with another couple. I can't remember the topic of conversation, but my friend said to his wife, "You can't understand because your parents weren't divorced." In that moment, I realized there is a bond between adults whose parents divorced because we know what it's like to live two parallel lives, to see our parents date, to live in conflict, to take sides, to help raise younger siblings, to feel grown up before our time, to (*fill in the blank here about your life*). I decided to create a survey for Adult Children of Divorce and had over 50 respondents answer 10 questions about what it was like for them to have divorced parents. The result turned into a blog series, *"Speaking Out; Voices of Adult Children of Divorce"* and now this book.

I used my own experience as an adult child of divorce and also my professional experience as a Divorce & Family Mediator to come up with the topics. My goal is for couples that are contemplating divorce to read this book and have a sense of what it will be like for their children if they make certain decisions. It's a "sliding doors" moment; if you choose door number one your future life can be harmonious as you raise your children separately but together, OR you choose door number two and you continue to make your children's lives unbearable as the two of you raise them separately and with fire and brimstone.

Studies show that 75% of children who come from divorced families do just fine. Children with less conflict in their lives (from divorce or other situations) will grow up and have an easier time with future relationships.

It doesn't matter how old you are when your parents divorce, in my opinion. It's always painful. It's a break, a rift, a severing of what was..." Lisa

My parents got divorced when I was 3 years old. I don't remember anything "before," only after, which was my normal life. Dad came over for dinner once a week, played "tickle monster" with us, and helped put us to bed. On Friday nights, he took us to his parents' house for Shabbat dinner and a visit, and when he stopped having roommates, we spent one-two nights a weekend at his apartment in Boston. The North End, Faneuil Hall, and the Aquarium were our playground. When we got older, and he lived in a house, we stayed with him three out of four weekends a month.

I have a memory of a dream where a suit hanging on a hanger came out of my closet, sat me on his lap on my bed, and told me that my parents were getting a divorce. I think that's the memory of what happened. A three year old doesn't understand what a divorce is, but maybe understands that her life will change forever.

My parents threw themselves a divorce party, fixed each other up, and worked well raising us together but separate, until my father got remarried to my "stepmonster"- not my current stepmother who has enriched my life in so many ways. The first stepmother was self-centered and unable to understand the workings of our family, or help my siblings and me feel comfortable in her presence.

There were times that came later when my parents weren't getting along. Out of respect to their privacy, I won't explain it here. Let's just say things became tense when I was in college, and it wasn't until my brother, sister, and I, each got married and they had to see each other again, that they become more cordial toward one another.

We were one of the few families in the 70's that had divorced parents, and I remember always feeling different. I was proud of my hip beautiful mother who worked as a volunteer advocate for welfare recipients in Massachusetts and later as a Tax Examiner for the state of

Massachusetts. She was and is my role model in how to live my life in support of others. I loved visiting with my dad and the friends I made in his community. He taught me to always "think twice before you speak once"- true words to live by. And I have a bonus parent, Deborah, who taught me about style, my appreciation for antiques, and, through her love, she helped me strengthen my relationship with my dad.

My experience with being a child of divorce is that no matter what I do that involves my parents, I constantly think about how the other one will feel (even writing the previous paragraph with praise for each of them). In high school, I was in charge of deciding which parent we'd spend holidays with, Mom's side or Dad's side. As a young woman getting married, I decided to walk down the aisle alone so as not to choose one (and I definitely wasn't walking between them). As a grown woman, I often don't include either of them so as not to have the awkwardness of being in the same space. Imagine spending your whole life navigating how not to hurt your parents' feelings through your actions and behaviors.

At the age of 45, I changed careers and became a Divorce Mediator after working in non-profit for 25 years. I truly believe it's my calling to help parents untangle their marriages and work toward better communication for their children's future. I teach the court-mandated parenting classes in Massachusetts, and when I tell people that my parents have been divorced for 48 years- they seem a little bit nervous. The point is, if you have children, and you get a divorce, you will be related forever. You'll continue to raise your kids together, watch them grow up, attend their weddings, have grandchildren, attend their birthday parties and life cycle events and so on and so on. **So the time of your divorce is really the opportunity to create a future for your family that works for you and your children**.

For more information on the author or to read her blogs go to:

www.divorcemediationabetterway.com

INTRODUCTION

In Massachusetts, parents going through a divorce are required to take a parenting class. I've been teaching this class one to two times a month for the last three years, and I find that when I share with the participants that I'm a child of divorce, they have a lot of questions for me. They want to know if their children are going to be okay, how long does it take to adjust, what can they do to make it work for their children, etc. These questions inspired me to ask questions of other adult children of divorce in the hope that parents getting divorced can learn from all of our experiences.

I had close to 50 respondents answer my questionnaire. The respondents were a broad range of ages, came from different backgrounds, live in all parts of the United States, and their parents divorced at different times in their lives. *Author's note: Several respondents have the same first name.*

CHAPTER 1

MEDIATION WORKS WHEN YOU TAKE THE TIME TO NURTURE YOUR DIVORCE

It may seem ironic that you would "nurture" a divorce, but mediation works best when both parties take the time to communicate with each other. Nurturing makes us think about love and care; divorce can feel full of hate and spite. My parents have been divorced for 48 years. And for those 48 years they've had to interact with each other through their three children and six grandchildren. They planned and attended our birthday parties, negotiated parenting time and holidays, and disciplined us together when we were growing up. Now that my siblings and I have kids, my parents and stepmother meet up frequently at our children's birthday parties, Bar/Bat Mitzvahs, school graduations, etc. Perhaps, someday they'll be together at their grandchildren's weddings.

When couples come to mediation, they've decided to work cooperatively to get through their divorce, but they should also plan to work cooperatively at **BEING** divorced.

People often think of a divorce as an event- "I was divorced on this day." If you have children, it's not a one-time event; it's an ongoing, complicated relationship. You will be "related" to your ex-spouse for the rest of your life. If you want that relationship to be full of venom and spite, that's your choice. If you want it to be full of mutual satisfaction and agreement on how you are raising your children, and how you are making your way in the world together, yet separate, then think about how you can nurture your relationship with your ex.

What does it mean to nurture your divorce? And how does one nurture a relationship with someone who may have really hurt you or whom you might actually even hate? It's going to look different for everyone and you may not be able to nurture it until after the divorce "event" takes place, and you've finished making all the decisions.

I want to share a few ideas:

1. During your separation, keep your children at the forefront of all your decisions and interactions with your ex-spouse.
2. Don't speak negatively about your ex in front

of your kids- they are part of each of you and will take everything personally.

3. Communicate: If you get a nasty email or text from your ex- respond with the "BIFF" method (BIFF stands for Brief, Informative, Friendly and Firm). Bill Eddy from the High Conflict Institute says, "How you respond to hostile communications may impact your relationships or the outcome of a case." When you respond to someone without engaging in the crossfire, it can change the entire tone of the correspondence. The good thing about emails is that you don't have to respond immediately. Take time to control your reaction. Hold onto your response for a day and reread it before responding if timing is allows.

4. Don't spend all your time looking in the rearview mirror. If you were driving and didn't look out the front window- you'd crash- and the same thing is true if you spend time rehashing all the bad memories and hurt feelings you have from your marriage. (Paraphrased from Joel Osteen)

5. Don't hold a grudge- someone wise once told me, when you hold a grudge it's like eating poison and hoping the other person will die. (Anonymous)

6. Don't be late with child support payments. Remember the money is to support your child, and if your ex doesn't have the money

they need, that will put more strain on your relationship and stress them out, which is not good for YOUR child.
7. Don't compete with your ex- your child knows and loves both of you and is internally aware of what you can and can't do emotionally and financially.
8. Don't be a "Disney World" parent- kids don't need to be entertained all of the time, in fact they'll respect you as a parent if you aren't always "fun."
9. Don't assume everything your ex says has an ulterior motive. Take the words at face value.

So while it might sound strange to nurture your divorce, in the long run, your whole family will benefit from it. Parents who see themselves as partners and work to raise their kids together (even though they are separate) will have less conflict in their own lives. And children whose parents are able to get along, will be happier and better adjusted than those whose parents are living in conflict. Mediation works best for those couples who are paying attention and want to nurture their relationship even after they're divorced.

CHAPTER 2

TELLING YOUR CHILDREN

"I was extremely shocked when my parents said they were getting divorced. I definitely cried and thought it was the worst thing in the world." **Isabella**

In class we discuss best practices for telling your children about the impending divorce. We stress the importance of both parents being present, to have a script, and to make sure you are on the same page. It was interesting to me that almost half of the respondents were told by only one of their parents, and some weren't told at all.

Jessica shared, *"My dad told my brother and me, 'I won't be coming home for a few days.' I really don't know why he said it like that but they made it sound very temporary. They never used the word 'divorce' when they first told us."*

Tovah said, *"They didn't really tell me. My mom*

tried to protect me and didn't want me to get hurt. I just figured it out."

I was curious if people were surprised when they found out their parents were getting a divorce. Almost half said yes.

Jonathan responded, *"At the time, I was absolutely floored. In hindsight, I guess I shouldn't have been that surprised."*

Susan said, *"Yes, I was shocked. I thought my parents had a great marriage. I was living away at college and had no idea my parents weren't getting along."*

Stephanie shared, *"Yes. I was quite surprised when they told me they were getting divorced. They had never argued or fought in front of us and (we) were confused."*

In the parenting classes, we teach that a "happy divorce" is better for children than a high conflict marriage. "Happy" in this case means that both parties have accepted their future as a divorced family. In the cases presented above, and perhaps it was the generation we lived in, the couples kept their conflict away from the children. Other people shared that they weren't surprised about the divorce since their parents were fighting all the time, and some were even relieved when their parents finally separated.

I was also curious about how the parents told their children they were getting divorced and how it felt to have divorced parents. There were a few themes that I found in the responses; some people felt ashamed or embarrassed, others felt that they had become more resilient as a result of their parents divorce, and others shared positive outcomes due to the divorce. In reading the responses to my questionnaire, I remembered my own childhood embarrassment at having divorced parents when all my friends came from "intact families."

Patrice thought, "*Socially, it was difficult at school because very few mothers were single at that time (1960s). I was openly excluded from social events and some children were not allowed by their parents to socialize with me. I was ashamed of my situation at school and in church situations.*"

Geoffrey shared, "*I remember feeling rushed and tense a lot of the time growing up. We never had very much money. I loved sports, but my mom had no real interest in them, so I wasn't very good. We'd always be the last to sign-up, I never knew what sort of equipment I should have, etc.*"

Liz responded, "*I was embarrassed. We were forced to sell our house and move. My mom had to get a job. I started a brand new school in a new city. My life turned upside down.*"

Anonymous, was raised by her dad, "*People had reactions to a single father raising an only daughter. They assumed my mom had died. It was strange for most people to think of a father being awarded primary custody, especially of a daughter.*"

Nancy became more resilient: "*I felt weird but my best friend's parents were also divorced and we formed a divorced parents club in my basement. We would talk about our feelings and rant. It was very therapeutic.*"

One of the things I remember feeling as a child was that we were still living in our "starter" home and all of my friends had moved to new neighborhoods in much bigger houses.

For some people, the divorce felt like a new normal and parents were able to get along. Before my dad married my first stepmother, my parents spent a lot of time co-parenting us, and spending time together. I even remember a trip to Florida where we spent the middle few days with my dad and the rest with my mom. My mom told me that my dad paid for her flight, including flying all of us from Miami to Orlando so she wouldn't have to drive.

Stephanie shared, *"At this point, so many of my friends' parents were getting divorced that it started to seem normal; I didn't really feel like I was the only one dealing with it."*

Patrice said, *"My parents always spoke highly of each other. They were friendly and we had holidays all together when I was older, including step-parents."*

Susan shared, *"One thing I'll give them, they never put me in the middle of whatever went on between them. I was smart enough to know my father never paid the dentist or my mother didn't invite his family, etc., but if I ever said something nasty about one in front of the other I was told to watch my mouth and parents were to be treated with respect."*

Jonathan has a positive outlook: *"I'm lucky my parents stayed close friends after they split. I've never had to take a side."*

I had clients come in recently and tell me that they thought they were "doing this divorce thing wrong". I asked them for clarification and they said they thought they were spending too much time together as a family and felt it would be confusing for their kids (ages 3 & 5). I assured them there's nothing wrong with spending time together if they're not fighting, even though they were splitting up. This was the "new normal" for their children.

CHAPTER 3

MOST DIFFICULT SITUATION
BEING A CHILD OF DIVORCE

"I felt abandoned and discarded...I'm always waiting for the other shoe to drop." **Tina**

Statistics show that 75% of children of divorce do fine, but the other 25% are directly affected by their parents' level of conflict post-divorce. It's important to remember that your children are made up of parts of both of you. If you disparage the child's other parent, it's as though you are taking a direct hit on your own child.

In my survey, I asked people what was the most difficult situation they faced as a result of their parents' divorce. My thoughts on this topic are that having divorced parents never ends. There are decisions that I make on a daily basis to make sure everything feels fair and equal. The responses below are raw and heartbreaking:

Mike said, *"The most difficult part is my father not really wanting to see us."*

Isabella shared, "*Difficult situations would be calling my father to remind him that the weekend was coming up and asking if he was gonna pick us up.*"

Tina wrote, "*I felt abandoned and discarded...I'm always waiting for the other shoe to drop. And I hate surprises- since the ultimate surprise was the abrupt end to my parents' marriage.*"

Liz, "*I felt so much pain. When my parents split, I was highly angry and took it out on my friends.*"

It's understandable that parents need emotional support while going through a separation, but it's important not to be dependent on your children for emotional support. There were times when I was a young adult that I wished my mom had a partner to help her.

I recommend having two or three people that you can call when you need to vent or cry. It's ok for your children to see you sad and know that you feel upset, however observing very strong emotion is difficult for children to process. It was difficult for **Lisa** who shared, "*The most difficult situation was feeling guilty about my mom being hurt by my wanting to still see him.*"

And for **Rachel** who hated holidays, "*Thanksgiving was the worst. I always felt like I had to choose where to be and was leaving someone out when I did.*"

Divorced children often feel pulled between their parents' new and different lifestyles. One parent may let them stay up later, eat different foods, or have chores for them. As a result, children often compartmentalize life with each parent.

Jay said, "*I think the hardest thing was getting mixed* *messages from each parent. Even though they were divorced, it seemed like they had different values and parenting styles and were not on the same page on most things."*

A number of people wrote that it is still hard to be in the same room with both parents at the same time. As an adult I've made the decision not to include my parents at certain events so we don't feel uncomfortable. They're never inappropriate- my siblings and I just like to keep them separate. In a way, it's like having two very different families and we don't know how to coexist in the same space.

Trine shared, *"When I got married it was very awkward having them in the same place."*

Ari said, *"...for years they couldn't be in the same room. If there was an event of some sort, there was tension. We worried for weeks if they would be able to get along. Sometimes they would act like the other one wasn't there; sometimes they would openly fight wherever we were."*

And life cycle events and celebrations became cause for worry and concern:

Faye remembers, *"My Bat Mitzvah...my Dad moved out just before my Bat Mitzvah. I remember telling my rabbi that without a happy family, I did not want to have a Bat Mitzvah.... But, my parents and the rabbi insisted and I did have one...."*

Anonymous said, *"Big life events were never easy. When I completed my college degree and my doctorate, I naturally wanted my family there to celebrate but I was* also anxious about having everyone in the same place. It's been easier to keep them separated in my mind."

Amy coached her parents on how to behave at her college graduation: "*I had to actually talk to each of them individually, before they traveled out to see me, and lecture them on behavior. I had to point blank tell them that this was one of the most important accomplishments in my life, and if they couldn't be civil not to bother coming and ruining it for me.*"

Divorced families need to make financial adjustments to support two homes. **Geoffrey** remembers a dramatic change in his family's financial situation, "*We were pretty middle class before the divorce. ... After the divorce we were POOR - government cheese and big patches on the knees of my pants poor. ...She was working as a teacher-aid and that year we put up a construction paper Christmas tree because our place was too small for a tree. I remember that my present that year was a plastic army helmet.*"

Dawn felt rejected by her father, "*... he would not walk me down the aisle with my mom at my wedding. I am Jewish and traditionally both (parents) walk the bride.*"

People think about their divorce in the here and now and not how it will affect them in the long term. I like to ask clients, "Think ahead to your child's wedding. Do you think you and your ex can stand on either side of your child and walk him/her down the aisle? And how do you think your child will feel standing between you?"

This question helps people to understand that they

will always be connected to one another through their children and how important it is to try to maintain a civil relationship despite how difficult it may be. Society no longer believes that a couple should stay married for the "sake of the children," but I strongly believe you can make your best effort to stay civil for your children's sake.

CHAPTER 4

HOW DID IT FEEL TO HAVE DIVORCED PARENTS?

***"There is not a birthday, wedding, or any event or holiday that is not filled with guilt about which parent to invite or distress by the emotional strain they create."* Nicole**

Many of the people I spoke with grew up in the 70s when it was less common to have divorced parents. Some felt like outcasts and that they didn't have anyone to speak to about what they were going through. The majority of people said how difficult it was to have divorced parents and that it continues to be difficult in their lives as adults. Many gave examples of events in their life when they had to split their time or attention: sports, dance recitals, graduations, etc.

Rita shared, *"It was always disjointing and somewhat discomforting when my mom and dad always had to sit apart at band concerts, and I had to meet them in different places at graduation."*

Similarly, **Lisa** said, "*I noticed it most when there were decisions to be made about who would go to certain life events -- graduations, etc -- and whose house I would go to for holidays.*"

Rhiannon felt there wasn't consistency in the way her parents parented her, "*The going back and forth wasn't nearly as bad as the fact that I knew they hated each other and was often put in the middle. There was no real consistency because they were always trying to impose their parenting styles, which would just break down the other's, and they seemed to sabotage each other out of spite. It was always very clear around holidays and in the summer when debates had to happen over where we would end up.*"

Eric responded, "*Not fun. Still notice it until today. Holidays and communications -- you have to report everything twice. Splitting time between loved ones is not fun. Not having them together as a couple means loneliness and heartbreak.*"

And **Amy** remembers, "*It was hard. I lived in a small town where everyone knew everyone and everything. It was also incredibly rare for people to get divorced back then and still a bit of a stigma. It was hardest during school functions. I was in drama, choir, marching band, and a few other activities. My parents couldn't get along in public so mostly I never invited them both to the same function.*"

There's also anger and embarrassment that kids feel about having divorced parents. For some it's being stuck in the middle of their ongoing arguments, for others it's sadness that one parent doesn't want to see them.

M shared, *"Divorce was not a usual thing back then and I felt embarrassed and different than my peers. I noticed during play-time, school time, night time, all the time."*

Heather felt, *"The hardest part was dealing with the animosity between them and feeling like being stuck in the middle all the time."*

TN said, *"In hindsight I guess I felt a degree of abandonment that has barely diminished to this day."*

Susan remembers, *"He never called. Never wanted to see me and not until I was 18 when I asked him to go for a drive with me did I ever ask him 'Why didn't you call me?'- He told me he never wanted (mom) to answer the phone."*

Stacey said, *"It was awful. I felt like I was the only one. I was lonely and sad. Both parents would fight on the phone; He did not want to pay for child support. It was ugly from the first day and never got better."*

Jessica shared, *"It felt different and more complicated than my friends who didn't have divorced parents. I didn't want to have to explain to anyone if I needed to be picked up or dropped off at a house that wasn't my own. It was a small town and everyone knew where I lived. I didn't want to explain that my dad lived with another family in another neighborhood."*

Liz felt she had to lie, *"My mom was sad a lot. I'll always remember a mom who lived across the street was* *prying and asked me if my Dad's car was in the garage. I lied and said yes. I was embarrassed. We were forced to sell our house and move. My mom had to get a job. I started a brand new school in a new city. My life turned upside down."*

I think a lot about people who have difficult relationships with their ex-spouses and how it affects their kids. If they had the opportunity to read what these adults feel today and felt as children, perhaps they would behave differently. There's no "right" way to be divorced, and I wish the grownups would spend more time understanding what it's like from the kids' perspectives.

CHAPTER 5

DIVIDED LOYALTY

"The divorce was officially referred to in our house as "the war." If something was gone and missing it was 'oh well, we lost it in the war.' **Amy**

Children of divorce may feel like they have two separate identities. The child may behave or act a certain way depending on which parent he or she is with at the time. Given the freedom to make your own rules, parents are setting up their homes the way you wish to for the first time. You may create new rules about bedtime, what to eat, what chores children do, etc. and this may vastly differ in each home. Children need to navigate their new landscape and understand what is expected of them in both of their homes. In this chapter, I wanted to explore how adult children of divorce felt in regard to divided loyalty between their parents and whether they felt they had to take sides with one parent or another.

For **Jessica**, there was fear of being disloyal to her mother, "*I never used the word "step-mother" until I was an adult. I thought that was a betrayal of my mother.*"

"G" said, "*Even now, at 31, I hesitate to talk about one in front of the other.*"

Similarly, **"B"** said, "*My defenses go up for either one when they mention something about one another or one another's family.*"

And **Traci** shared, "*To this day, when my mom "bad-mouths" my dad, it makes me uncomfortable. Now that I'm older and more confident, I have no issues asking her to stop.*"

Susan found some positive in the division: "*Would I have been independent if I didn't need to divide myself between parents, quite literally? Who knows?*"

For some children, their parents might not have asked them to take a side, but because of the circumstances around the divorce, the child sensed that they had to out of loyalty. This seems to correlate with the child wanting to protect the parent who was more "wounded" by the divorce.

Take **Kristen**, she felt "*We will forever be on our mom's side. She is the one who selflessly and tirelessly took care of us and did everything for us.*"

And **Isabella**, "*I was always a daddy's girl but living with my mom I felt like I had to have her side. I felt like if they were arguing and I would take my mom's side so she* wouldn't be mad. She never did get mad but I didn't want to hurt her feelings."

Faye felt similarly, too, "*I always took the side of my mom because she took such great care of us... I wanted to protect her and show my appreciation for her.*"

Lisa's mom let it go, but **Lisa** felt guilty, "*...there's always guilt. I was absolutely devoted to my mom. She had been wronged, right? ... I knew it was upsetting for my mom but to her credit and incredible strength, love, and concern for me, she gritted her teeth and didn't stand in my way.*"

While some people said that they had to take sides with one parent, another woman (also named **Lisa**) said, "*I didn't have to take a side, but at the time of their separation and divorce, I sided with my father. In retrospect, I now have a more balanced view of the situation, but at that time I was more upset with my mother's out of control, unpredictable, irrational behavior, and so empathized with my father's decision to move out of the house.*"

Jessica also worried that she had to choose her dad's side, but it was based in fear, "*My Dad always made me feel like I had to choose sides. I was so scared of him that I didn't trust anything he said, so I never chose his side for sure.*"

And **Heather** said, "*Yes, I did take my dad's side because he was more vocal to me about the situation which resulted in me being very upset with my mother. As an adult, I see that he shouldn't (have) done that but he didn't have the capacity to handle it any other way.*"

Angela was torn apart by it, *"My mother tried to make us take her side. It was a gut-wrenching experience."*

Geoffrey thought he was protecting his dad, *"I'm still not sure why I stood up for him, but I think I sensed how sad and uncomfortable he was picking us up and dropping us off. I think he didn't know how to overcome this."*

I think there are "rules" that children of divorces with conflict start to follow when they become grownups. I rarely mention one of my parents to the other and definitely would never disparage one of them in conversation with the other. There is no one who teaches us to navigate these conversations, except the feeling you get in the pit of your stomach when you hear one of them talking about the other. It may not be negative; it just feels wrong.

These responses show a side of hurt by children whose parents were distracted by their own emotions around the divorce and may have been unable to see beyond them to the effect their behavior was having on their children.

CHAPTER 6

CAUGHT IN THE MIDDLE

> *"I always had to choose where to be and wherever I was, I felt like I was betraying the other parent..."* **Rachel**

In addition to taking sides, many children feel "caught in the middle" of their parents. For others, there's the feeling of being pulled between their parents. Being caught in the middle includes hearing one parent complain about the other. When a child (or a grownup) hears their parent being disparaged, it's like they are being criticized themselves. As an adult, I don't like to hear my parents talk about the other one. It doesn't matter if it's an innocuous comment; I am prepared for battle.

Eric shared, *"Hearing complaints from one about the behavior of the other was never nice. It puts you in an impossible position to hear them out while not wanting to at all."*

Stacey lived in the middle of the anger. "*When I was with my father, he would talk sh*t about my mom. When I got home, if I had fun with my father, my mom called him Disneyland Dad and got mad at us. She would bad mouth him and vice versa.*"

Heather felt similarly, "*The hardest part was dealing with the animosity between them and feeling like being stuck in the middle all the time.*"

Holidays are particularly difficult for divorced families. Children may miss being with one side of the family, worry about choosing which parent to be with, feel sad for the parent who was alone, or overwhelmed by too many family events. There were years that we had Thanksgiving dinner with one side and showed up to the other side for dessert. Everyone wanted to know why we weren't eating — we were so full!

Liz remembered being sad for her dad, "*I do remember feeling so sad at holidays when my Dad was alone. It was very painful for me. My Dad began to fall apart physically and the responsibility was enormous.*"

Rachel didn't like the choice, "*I did, however, always hate Thanksgiving (still don't love it) because I always had to choose where to be and where ever I was, I felt like I was betraying the other parent. Why did they make me choose? I still feel that way now.*"

Eric didn't like having more than one holiday, "*Holidays and communications -- you have to report everything twice. Splitting time between loved ones is not fun. Not having them together as a couple means loneliness and heartbreak, even if they both were alone with the divorce.*"

Lisa said, "*Holidays weren't hard because it was never a question that my brothers and I would spend every single one with our mom. He would ask from time to time but never expected it. He knew what he did and that it wouldn't be right.*"

Traci didn't come home, "*Since I was in school in Boston, and my parents lived in NJ, I rarely came home. I felt I needed to split my time evenly. It became stressful for me.*"

Some parents put their children in the middle by asking them to give the other parent something. It's important not to put your children in the middle of your arguments or ask children to be your "messengers" to deliver information, child support, mail, etc.

Ari felt like a messenger, "*Our parents, as is probably common, often used us. "Tell your dad that..." "Tell your mother that she still owes me..." They were warned not to do that, but that's just how it goes sometimes.*"

And so did **Jay**, "*I became the intermediary shuttling information back and forth between them (although more so from my mother to my father). Because of the strain in their relationship, it seemed like my mother came to everything at school and my father didn't. I assume that was because that was the way she wanted it. It was also hard sharing information with him only seeing him a couple of times a week.*"

Some children feel guilty about their circumstance and feel caught in the middle of the family divorce dynamic.

Tina felt guilty because she ended up with two

moms and her sisters lived with her dad, *"Well, it was fun for me cause I got my mom. I got my own room for the first time and I got to decorate it. I got to live with two moms, which was fun... I experienced (and still in my adult life it translates) a lot of guilt, as I knew my sister was devastated that mom didn't "pick her". I was taken from my three sisters and my life was never the same."*

You can see from the examples in this chapter that it's never a good idea to ask children to pass messages or deliver alimony/child support checks. I would take it one step further and say that even if it's difficult to communicate with each other, find the best method to keep your children away from the crossfire. We live in a technological era and texting and emailing can be easier than a difficult phone call.

CHAPTER 7

NAVIGATING THE HOLIDAYS IN A DIVORCED FAMILY

Let's talk about the holidays- if you are going through a divorce, the holidays can be an emotional time for you. Whether it's your first year without your kids, or the 10th year without them, it's difficult to face the holidays alone.

If it's the first year, you may be feeling isolated and alone. You might worry that your kids are going to miss you. Preparation is key.

Here are 10 tips for spending the holidays alone:

1. If you won't have your kids with you, ask your family to alert other guests so you don't have to answer over and over about where they are - or have your Aunt Alice say, "Aren't you lucky to have a kid-free day!"

2. If you attend church or synagogue, arrange to go with a friend so you don't have to sit alone.
3. Bring your own car. If it gets too emotional for you, you can leave.
4. Have three friends on speed-dial; they will be your lifelines if you need support.
5. Set up a time to talk or text with your kids so they know you're thinking of them while you are separate.
6. Have a plan- don't stay home and have a pity party.
7. Make sure you ask for support from friends and family- think about what it is that YOU need.
8. Take care of yourself- go for a walk, a run, a yoga class, watch the game, or read a book.
9. Sign up for the local Turkey Trot. You can walk or run but you'll see lots of people.
10. Three words – Black Friday Shopping.
11. Volunteer at a soup kitchen.

If you have a friend or family member going through a divorce, you can offer support in many ways. Reach out and let them know you understand this is a difficult time for them and ask what you can do to help. Feel free to join your friend for any of the activities listed above. And the best thing you can do is be a good listener- try not to offer advice and just listen.

CHAPTER 8

"PARENTIFICATION"

"At the age of 10 (when my parents separated), I became my mother's confidant." **T.S.**

Every time I tried to write about "Parentification," something came up and I was grateful for the distraction. I think it's because the idea came from the realization that my siblings and I often played a "parenting role" with each other. It can be easier to rely on your sibling and not have to choose a parent for guidance. The best example in my life is that my older brother (by two years) moved me into college. It was easier than deciding between my parents.

Parentification is the process of role reversal whereby a child is obliged to act as parent to his or her own parent.

Parentification can also be called "Child Support," and I'm not talking about money. In this case, it's cautionary for parents not to rely on their kids for emotional support. When kids see parents hurting, it's a natural instinct to want to help. For example: A child may cancel their weekend plans to stay home with a parent who is sad. Parents need to find their own support networks: friends, family, therapists, etc. and not burden their children with this difficult role.

Two distinct modes of Parentification have been identified: Instrumental Parentification and Emotional Parentification. Instrumental Parentification involves the child completing physical tasks for the family, such as looking after a sick relative, paying bills, or providing assistance to younger siblings that would normally be provided by a parent. Emotional Parentification occurs when a child or adolescent must take on the role of a confidant or mediator for (or between) parents or family members.

Stacey took on the role of "Instrumental Parentification" -- she essentially took care of her younger brother. *"Yes, I was the PARENT!!! My mom was such a freaking mess that from the time I was 4 years old I was taking care of my baby brother. She was always crying, unable to function, suicidal, messed up and I was the one who handled everything. At 14, I had a full time job to take care of her and my brother. Even though she passed in 1986, I still take care of my brother as he is really crazy from all the childhood sh*t."*

Stephanie felt responsible for her dad, *"My dad is more of a fun child himself and I had to take a lot of the responsibility with making sure he didn't forget things, and make sure we were on time for other things."*

Geoffrey felt the burden of responsibility for his younger brother as well, *"My mom suffered from anxiety* *and depression. She took pills for her condition and I hated being alone and taking care of my brother when she was sleeping from the pills or when she was out on a date."*

I was responsible for making sure that my younger sister's hair was braided before we got to my grandparents. I also decided which side we would go to for holidays when I was in high school.

Jessica and Amy took on Emotional Parentification, feeling that they had to support their parents.

"Yes, I believe I was Parentified. When my parents got a divorce my Mom heavily leaned on me emotionally although I was only eight years old. She was devastated when I became a teenager and started to spread my wings. It was hard on me because I wanted to live a normal life as a youth, but she wanted me around all the time because she was lonely." **Jessica**

"In my family case it was emotional parentification... almost like we became the sounding board or the dumping ground for the emotions when a therapist would have been best." ***Amy***

In **T.S.'s** case, there was inappropriate sharing from mom to child regarding intimacy and their sex life. *"At the age of 10 (when my parents separated), I became my mother's confidant. She would tell me about how she and my dad never had intimacy.... how he cheated on her with a married woman with a cocaine addiction... how she questioned his sexuality... how she once cheated on him with a man she met at work to get affection... how my dad was verbally and physically abusive towards her, etc....*

This pattern of her confiding in me about adult issues continued through the years."

It seems straightforward that as a parent you shouldn't rely on your child for emotional support, but when you are in the midst of divorce, it's an emotional roller coaster. Try to take time to think about what you're asking your children to do, and if they volunteer to stay home with you instead of seeing friends, reassure them that you're ok.

CHAPTER 9

HOW CUSTODY ARRANGEMENTS EVOLVED OVER TIME

"We would eat brunch and get a carwash. I don't think he knew what to do as a solo parent." **Ari**

One definition of custody is "the right of determining residence, protection, care, and education of a minor child or children, especially in a divorce or separation." It's interesting how custody has shifted throughout the years. In the early part of the previous century, men were awarded custody since women couldn't own property. Having no place to live when they got divorced, women went back to live with their parents and the children stayed with the father. In the 1960s through the early 2000's, women were primarily awarded custody, with fathers typically seeing their kids on alternating weekends and perhaps one night during the week for dinner.

In the past 10 years there's been a shift toward

50/50 parenting time, where the children spend close to equal parenting time with each parent. There are a number of factors at play here. As women moved into the workforce and some became the primary earners, fathers now have the opportunity to be more involved in their children's day-to-day lives. Studies show the importance of spending time with both parents, and judges are granting this type of parenting time (formerly known as custody).

I was curious about the kind of arrangements people had after their parents got divorced and how they felt about their arrangement. For some, it was difficult and messy, with a move and a loss of friends. They were far from their other parent and felt a loss of environmental stability. For others, it was positive; particularly when they got to make the choice about where to go for weekends or holidays.

Rhiannon said, *"It was a mess...those were always splintered with periods of fighting and trying to get sole custody or chip at each other's time. Holidays were supposed to alternate as well."*

Rita shared, *"The custody that was arranged was half and half... I remember crying about not being with my mom and having to be with my dad, and my dad just kept telling me that I had to be with him or something like that."*

Jay had the typical arrangement and the difficulties that came with it, *"My mother had custody of us and we saw my father one evening a week for dinner and stayed over at his apartment one evening on the weekend. It [was]* difficult on me for a number of different reasons... There were no cell phones or texting back then so keeping in touch was even harder than it is today."

Stephanie remembers having to pack a bag, "*We had to always make sure we didn't forget to bring anything with us each time we switched from parent to parent. They always had different meeting spots and different times and we never really knew when and where we'd be.*"

Amy's dad wanted custody and had trouble finding a lawyer to fight for it, "*... this was back in the day when mothers were basically always given custody regardless of if they were a fit parent or not. My dad was actually turned away by divorce lawyers when they found out he planned on fighting for custody.*"

Mike and Isabella felt the loss of the other parent:

Mike shared, "*We lived with my mother and saw my father sometimes on the weekends. I hated it because we only saw my father every once in a while and he had no interest in seeing us.*"

And **Isabella** said, "*I definitely had a hard time because I wanted to see my dad more. Sometimes we didn't see him on the weekend and it would make me sad.*"

Amanda's mom didn't want her spending time with her father, "*I visited dad every weekend. He would pick me up and drop [me] off. She hated that! I would have to clean the whole house and [do] laundry before I could go and it was terrible coming back. One time she locked me out. I had to go to a store and call dad. He came back to get me.*"

Lisa was older at the time of divorce and felt guilty,

"I was absolutely devoted to my mom. She had been wronged, right? .... I wasn't ready to lose the only dad I knew. I knew it was upsetting for my mom but to her credit and incredible strength, love, and concern for me, she gritted her teeth and didn't stand in my way."

The non-custodial parent so often doesn't know what to do with their kids. They don't have the toys, books, and equipment at their home and so the kids felt like visitors, and the parents felt that they had to entertain them the whole time they were together.

Geoffrey said, *"When my dad didn't have us stay with him he would often visit for an afternoon and we would go bowling or go for a hike, he called it a "walk-of-adventure." I think we'd just sort of wander around for a while. Eventually, we worked out an arrangement where we [would] visit his house every month or so and visit my paternal grandfather's house on other visitation weekends."*

Ari felt obligated to see his dad, *"We just wanted to spend time with friends, and now we had to spend half our weekends either in my dad's crummy apartment or later in his house 20 miles away. If there was a birthday party or something else it became that much more complicated. My dad wanted his time to be special, but (unlike in the movies) he didn't plan big exciting things. We would eat brunch and get a carwash. I don't think he knew what to do as a solo parent."*

Today, I hear from parents how the gain of having individual time with their children allows them to make decisions and spend time parenting how they want to. When each parent sets up a home and has a place for children to do homework or bring friends over, they're less inclined to feel that they need to run around like a "Disney" parent. Thinking about how to make your house a home and including your kids in age appropriate decisions- like picking out a new comforter or what color to paint the walls, helps the children to acclimate to the change as well.

CHAPTER 10

THINK OF IT LIKE A BUSINESS RELATIONSHIP

There are a number of sitcoms on TV these days that are trying (and sometime succeeding) in showing the lighter, funnier side of parenting together (but separate). I tell myself I'm watching for "research" and actually, sometimes they're spot on.

Recently I was watching "Single Parents," on ABC, and Will's ex-wife, Mia, had swooped in from her worldwide travels and saving the world, for their daughter's birthday. Will's friend Angie tries to help Will cope with Mia's interference in Will's rules by telling him- (paraphrase)- "Listen, it's a business and your company is 'Sophie, Inc.' so deal with Mia like she's one of your colleagues and you have to get along in the workplace."

This is actually something I talk about with clients quite a bit. We behave the worst with people we care about and who are close to us. Could you imagine sending an email to a colleague with accusations and expletives about why they didn't refill the coffee pot this morning?

Dealing with your ex like a business partner can play itself out in a lot of ways.

Communication- when you email, text, or make a phone call, think of it as a business transaction.

In person-if you don't sit near your ex at a sporting event, think about moving closer to them. When your child scores a goal or comes off the field, they won't be torn about where to head first.

Calendar- use a shared electronic calendar for your parenting plan. Older kids can have access to it and know where they're headed and when.

Holidays- Think about what's best for your children- if your ex's "Aunt Alice" is going to be visiting for Thanksgiving and it's not his/her year, be generous about switching.

In person- even when your child is upset about something with your ex- help her figure out how to advocate for herself. Don't immediately get on the phone to "fix" things.

So as you move on into a co-parenting space, think about your ex like a colleague, and your product is your child. You want that product to be the very best that s/he can be. By reducing the conflict between you and your ex, your product will improve daily.

CHAPTER 11
ADVICE FROM THE EXPERTS

"You are getting divorced, your kids are not!"
Nicole

So you're getting a divorce- feeling ashamed, embarrassed, worried about messing up your kids? It's so hard to make an adult decision about your marriage and not worry about how it will affect your children. And now you and your spouse will each have more control over how you parent, what you do in your own home, and how you spend time with your kids. Here's some advice from the experts -- adults whose parents divorced. Take it from them; they've lived through it already.

Nicole advises, *"You are getting divorced your kids are not! SO you need to figure out how to be adults and keep the FAMILY together. They should not have to choose,* *they should not have to white knuckle every holiday because YOU decided to move on."*

Jessica said:
"1. *Don't fight in front of them.*
2. *Don't speak negatively about the other parent.*
3. *Try to keep them in school consistently.*
4. *Get them counseling even if you don't think they need it. Don't use the "kids are resilient" excuse. They are not as resilient as you think."*

Liz stresses communication and honesty, *"Open communication is key! Honesty is so important. Therapy can be helpful for the kids too."*

Emotional stability for parents is really important. Make sure you are getting the support that you need to take care of yourselves. I tell clients to have a list of 2-3 people they can call who will be available to listen.

Don't use your children as weapons. Keep your kids at the forefront of all your decisions.

Rhiannon shared, *"Think of the children, seriously. You can be angry and hurt and betrayed and whatever* *emotions you want, but do not be petty and snide and try to destroy each other's image. ...It's fine to argue or whatever around the kids, but don't pull them from their homes in the middle of the night, don't tell them you're monitoring the other parent's phone calls, and please never put them in a situation where they have to watch a parent get in trouble with the law. Do not sabotage each other for the sake of getting what you want; it will only serve to traumatize your child and make it impossible for them to trust either of you."*

Environmental stability is equally as important- as much as you can do to keep routines -- school, bedtime, etc. -- the same, the easier it is for kids to adjust to the many changes that are happening in your family.

Rita expressed, *"Please understand that we're going through just as much as you are. Our foundation, our family, is breaking apart. Please realize that we're having trouble too and don't hold it against us. When everything is changing, please try to be a rock for us, try to give us some stability in this unstable time. Try to understand where we're coming from."*

It's important that children have contact with both parents. Today, more and more families have 50/50 shared parenting time. This wasn't the case in the 60s to 90s.

. . .

Geoffrey said "Make sure that both parents fulfill their responsibilities to their children. This means being physically, financially and emotionally present. Fathers are often pushed out of the picture either by moms making visitation difficult or by their own guilt. Don't let this happen."

HJ shared, "I certainly haven't figured out the part of not causing shock, but I do think it is possible to stay very connected with our children during hard times. Make yourself more available, play more games, watch more movies together, set up special times with each of them to do something just the two of you."

Letting kids share how they feel is important. Keeping communication open for them to ask questions and talk is a gift you can give your kids. I find the best place to talk with kids is in the car, you don't need to make eye contact and you can have their full attention. Don't be afraid to ask them to put it away their phone.

Patrice said, "Let them be upset. My mother often told me that the divorce had not upset me because I was too young to know whatever's happening. I grew up trying to believe that but it wasn't true that it had not hurt me. She thought of the divorce as an event, but I experienced it as a lifelong condition."

. . .

Geoffrey felt, *"Give them opportunities to bring up hard feelings by paying good attention to them, helping them laugh so that the tears may come naturally."*

Tovah shared, *"Try to keep your kids out of it. I think my mom did the best she could. Protect your kids especially if they're young. Ask them what they want and consider their feelings first."*

Remember getting a divorce is not an event; it's a new configuration of your life and you're navigating it while your children are growing up, which is complex. You can, and should, nurture your divorce relationship.

CHAPTER 12

MORE ADVICE FROM THE EXPERTS

"Love your children like nothing else matters and always be honest." **Stacey**

We've all heard people say that they stayed together for the kids. Unfortunately, if there's conflict in the home, then it's not better for the kids to have married parents. They'll have to learn how to navigate a divorced family. My best advice-I think it's important to not compete with the other parent for love and attention from your kids and not talk negatively about them in front of your kids.

Lisa A. shared, *"Don't assume that 'staying together for the children' is a good idea. Try to establish frequent contact for kids with other family members who can provide the loving support that they may not be getting as much of from their parents. Do not assume that teens that want to be independent are actually ready to be indepen-*

dent, just because it is more convenient for you as a single or separated parent."

Don't disparage the other parent. Your children are half of each of you and when you speak negatively or emphasize "your mom" or "your dad," it's really painful to your kids.

Rhiannon said, *"The divorce was never a problem for me; it was the feeling that these two people actively wanted to kill each other (which I heard, verbatim, on at least one occasion) and that they would stop at nothing to make sure we held the same contempt."*

Jessica suggested, *"I would ask them to try as hard as possible to keep their opinions of their spouse and their dealings with their spouse from their children. They should let their children retain as much normalcy and regularity in their lives as possible. They should never talk about financial arrangements or other grievances with children."*

CN agrees, *"Make it your JOB not to disparage your children's other parent! Bitch to your friends (out of earshot, please), talk to your therapist, smoke a joint, have a cocktail, whatever you need to do, do it. Just don't badmouth your kids' other parent. That is wrong on every level and grossly unfair to your child (makes them question what they think they know about their world, whom to trust, whom to believe) as well as to your ex spouse. (S)he is just as much (genetically, anyway) your child's parent as you are. Don't ruin your kids' life out of selfish spite."*

Isabella hated the arguments, *"I would tell other*

people to not fight in front of your children and just get along for the children. If you aren't getting along, put on a fake smile and don't let the child feel like something is wrong. My parents fought in front of me and I always thought it was my fault or stressed about how I could fix it. If they would have just got along for us, I feel like the stress would not have been there. Keep communication with your child. Ask them how they feel about what's going on. I wish they had talked to me more."

JD advises, *"Work out your adult problems as and between adults. Don't share the details with your kids. Reassure them that none of it is their fault - this is between you and the other parent. Tell them that you will work everything out and will still work together to take care of them - then do that! Never share your laundry list of the other parent's faults with your kids. They have the right and they need to love and respect both parents."*

Amy said, *"Keep your children out of it. Keep your petty fights and "bs" to yourselves. Your children see more and understand more than you will ever realize. No matter how hard it is, how wronged you were, be the better parent. I saw what my mother did to my father, I know first hand the nightmare she put him through, but he never badmouthed her in front of me. He always reminded me that she was still my mother and that she still loved me in her own way. Looking back as an adult, I can only imagine how hard that was for him, but it makes me respect him that much more and it makes me appreciate that he tried for me, even when she wasn't willing to."*

Lisa B.'s mom was a role model. *" I actually would*

use my mom as the example. She was the injured party and yet she never badmouthed him. She stayed positive and made sure we appreciated what he did for us and meant to us all. That's astounding!"

Reinforce over and over again to your kids that it's not their fault. Younger children have "magical thinking" and believe that they have control over situations in their lives just because they thought about it. And don't put your kids in the middle.

Jay suggests, *"I would say that all parents should tell their kids that the divorce is not their fault and that both parents love them very much. Then follow it up with actions that reinforce that belief: don't put your kids in the middle, don't make them choose between one parent and the other, and don't talk badly about the other parent. While it may not have worked out for you two as a couple, you are still the parents of your children and you should both be able to share many occasions with your children and not have one parent there or the other because you can't stand to be in a room together."*

You can be more than civil; you can still be a family. There are couples that are definitely better as friends and after the divorce they find a way to spend time together.

Trine shared, *"Things started out great after the divorce. No one ever back talked each other and we would have dinner together and go on vacation together. It was a wonderful setup. I would encourage parents to try to remain civil even after a stepparent comes into the picture. They say that love dies but jealousy lasts forever and I believe that is true with divorced couples."*

Nancy had a similar situation, *"My parents would meet and do things together that involved us kids, would talk and meet and be together on all birthdays, mitzvahs, and events. We still all get together often for holidays at each other's houses. Remain friends as much as possible for the kids."*

Don't compete with the other parent for love and attention. As my brother says, "Love is not a zero sum game- your kids have enough love for both of you."

Ari said, *"... They shouldn't use the children as pawns, telling the kids what to say to the other parent. But I also realize how difficult this is. In a way, you want to win your kid's affection. You're now in competition for it. You want to paint the other as a bad guy. It makes sense, but it is wrong and extremely hurtful to the kids."*

Jasmine agrees, *"Don't make your child feel guilty for having a relationship with the other parent. Especially once they reach adulthood, that relationship is their business, not yours."*

Learning from adults who experienced divorce as children or young adults so that you don't make the same mistakes or blunders is important. Your divorce relationship is unique and so is your family.

CHAPTER 13

POSITIVE OUTCOMES OF DIVORCE AS FELT BY ADULT CHILDREN OF DIVORCE

***"It was the best thing that could have happened…"* Tovah**

If you are unhappy in your marriage, then perhaps the divorce can bring some positive to your lives and the lives of your children. The majority of people in my survey felt that some good had come out their parents' divorce. Four of the families got away from violent situations, five said there was less tension in their parents' relationship with less fighting, and 14 wrote about a parent finding new love, relationships, and/or marriage.

Many people wrote about the strength and positive changes that they saw in their mothers. Moms grew stronger in character because they were single and were role models for daughters. My own mother who felt that she grew up as a stereotypical "princess," became a "Women's Libber" and learned how to fix the toilet, change the thermostat, and invest in the stock market.

HJ said, "*My mother became stronger, and grew in many ways. She began dating and eventually married my stepfather, who was an incredibly warm and caring man who loved all of us very, very much.*"

Patrice recognized the strength of her mother as a single mother. "*My mother was awesome as a single mom. I don't think she'd have come into her self and found feminism if she'd been married.*"

Lisa learned from her mom. "*She (my mother) showed us to go after what you want, not to give up, to keep a positive attitude regardless of sh*tty circumstances, surround yourself with people who love you for friendship and support, and to BOUNCE...Be Resilient...*"

"*It was the best thing that could have happened and I'm grateful that I lived with my mom. It is because of her that I have good values, am a good person, educated, and have a good job as a teacher,*" said **Tovah**.

Relationships with fathers improved too: these women felt that they had more time to spend with their dads:

Trine said, "*My relationship with my father grew stronger since we had more dedicated time together. Our family life was very stable and comfortable after the divorce. There was no more fighting or arguing and everyone got along better.*"

Amy shared, "*There was so much less fighting, anger, and violence in the house. The house I lived in with my dad became a home and safe haven for me again. My relationship with my dad also got much better. We were honest and open with each other about things.*"

A few people wrote about their resolve for the future of their own relationships and how important it is to work things out.

Anonymous felt, *"I am very close to my father, and I am careful with my heart. I am marrying a wonderful man, and I took my time in finding him because I only intend on doing this once. Everyone says that, but we took our time getting engaged and have worked hard to have excellent and honest communication."*

Jay said, *"It also made me realize that divorce was not going to be an option for me. I was going to find someone I love, get married and stay happily together, even if there were some trying times that we had to go through."*

Amy felt similarly, *"I got married very young, 18 years old, but I went into with the mindset that if things got bad we would try to work it out, not just walk away. I just celebrated my 15-year wedding anniversary.*

One of the strongest positives that people wrote about is their own self-growth and awareness because they have divorced parents. Also, they felt they deserved to be happy in a relationship. I've been married for 22 years, and we spend time working on our marriage all the time to make sure we are in sync with our needs and desires in the relationship and as parents.

Traci said, *"I have since learned that we all deserve to be ourselves and deserve to be happy. And healthy relationships -- partnerships-- can exist."*

Jessica learned, *"I have deep compassion for others, which I don't think I would have if I didn't go through such a hard situation."*

Stephanie wouldn't be who she is today. *"I guess if my parents never got divorced I wouldn't be where I am today. Never would have changed schools, found my passion, met my husband, went to art school and started my own business."*

"CN" *recognized that the divorce was good for both of his parents, "They both eventually had a chance to be who they were meant to be, with significant limitations due to age, illness, and financial constraints. But each found new or previously dormant parts of themselves and let them blossom. It was glorious to see!"*

It's clear that a divorce you can nurture is better than an unhappy marriage. While not all divorces result in happiness, there is usually acceptance about the situation. In these scenarios, many of the parents were able to move on and find new romance or happiness with him/herself.

CHAPTER 14

POSITIVE OUTCOMES OF
DIVORCE - PART TWO

"Maybe, by them getting a divorce, it saved their friendship." Jonathan

For some people, their parents' divorce lessened the conflict; moms became more independent, and maybe one or both parents found new partners. People reported becoming more resilient when they were children, able to handle what life threw at them, and perhaps they chose their future partners more carefully.

Rhiannon said, *"They're both better off just being friends and not having to share in responsibilities. It's let my mom be more free and creative and given my dad a better opportunity to explore his true self."*

Rita learned her parents are real people, *"When you go through a divorce and that brings out their real selves, their flaws and differences, you realize that even they are only human. Although to many (people) divorce may seem like something that defines a person negatively and that* *person is forevermore flawed, but I can't help but feel like I came out of the divorce stronger, and wiser, more defined."*

Susan A. also saw her parents grow after the divorce, *"I really got to know my parents as separate people rather than as part of my family. I realized how different they were from one another. My dad was always on the go, type A personality. My mom needed to slow down and become her own person."*

HJ saw her mother blossom, *"I am very grateful that my mother was able to have the strength and resolve to end the marriage."*

"As a teen I always believed my parents marriage had 'failed' and I was determined not to make the same mistakes they did. I guess I made different mistakes because I still wound up divorced! Actually, what I learned is that just because a marriage doesn't last, doesn't mean getting married was a mistake. I have a better appreciation for the fact that my parents were better off apart and I learned a lot from their divorce that I applied to my own." **Michael**

Susan B's, Isabella's, and JD's parents also found new partners:

Susan B: *"They became much happier people -- especially when they found their new, wonderful spouses."*

Isabella: *"They both seemed a lot happier after, they both found people who they love and are extremely happy with. They are completely different people now."*

JD: *"They both went on to find love and happiness with another."*

Amy was happy for the violence to end, *"It was*

rough to adjust after mom left, but there was so much less fighting, anger, and violence in the house. The house I lived in with my dad became a home and safe haven for me again. My relationship with my dad also got much better. We were honest and open with each other about things."

Jessica had a number of positives: *"1. I got out of an abusive home. 2. My Mom raised me in the church, so I was surrounded by loving people who cared about me. 3. I wasn't raised by my father's twisted view of the world. 4. I have deep compassion for others, which I don't think I would have if I didn't go through such a hard situation."*

A new family member is a positive for **Dawn;** *"The best thing was gaining a step-sister who is to this day my best friend. Too bad we live far apart. She is the sister I prayed for at age 3. It would have been far worst to live with parents that fought all the time and were dysfunctional."*

Susan C. had a lot of positive outcomes in her own life, *"I am totally independent. Can do (or teach myself to do) almost anything, travel anywhere, pay my own way, live my own life. I am upfront and sometimes too honest (with others, anyway), have realistic expectations about truth, money, relationships, etc."*

CN is grateful for her parents; *"I bet a lot of people have revelations about learning that they, or their mothers or their fathers 'really can make it on their own'. But I already - always - knew that. I had great parents who taught me that from day one!"*

Kelly's brothers made better choices, *"My mother*

became a strong, independent person, and taught all of us to be the same way. My brothers all became great dads and husbands, because they wanted to be different than the way he was."

In our country, almost half of marriages end in divorce. Most people I know feel that some good came out of their marriage (the best thing is usually their children), and if you are able to come out of the marriage with more independence, a renewed sense of self, or a better parent, then is that a "failure?" I think we need to re-imagine what is success and failure in a marriage, and perhaps the divorce is simply the next chapter in your life?

CONCLUSION

If you're separating or getting a divorce, my hope is that reading this book will help you better understand how to handle many circumstances that arise before, during, and after your divorce. By hearing directly from people who have experienced being the children of divorce and how it affected them both as children and into adulthood, you can decide what kind of divorce you want. Even though you don't have any control over your ex, you have control over yourself and your actions. While you may not need my services, I'd be delighted if you'd share my book with others in your life who might gain insight from what they find in these pages.

In my mediation practice, I work with couples to amicably separate and prepare for their divorce. This includes creating a Parenting Plan that works for their unique family, figuring out how to divide assets and liabilities, and talking about their goals for the divorce itself and life post-divorce. When you think about being related to each other FOREVER, because you're still parenting your children together, you can see how you might want the relationship to be going forward.

When I trained to be a mediator, I didn't know how much I would love this work. If I've made the difference in even one child's life, then I've reached my goal. In my own experience with divorced parents, there were times that my parents were best friends, and times that they were bitter enemies. It shaped who I am, for better or worse, and as the middle child of divorced parents, I can negotiate with the best of them.

I decided to become a public speaker when I was asked to present at a networking group. I realized that I have a knack for standing up in front of people and engaging them in a topic. Let me know if you'd like me to come share with your community. I can be reached at jodycomins@me.com.

With blessings and gratitude,

Jody

ACKNOWLEDGMENTS

I'd like to thank my heart and soul, Mike Schnur, and our two amazing daughters, Talia and Elizabeth, for supporting me in all that I endeavor, including my career shift at age 46. My brother, Michael Comins, and my sister, Jami Schultz, for their editing contributions and for corroborating my memories of growing up in the 70s with divorced parents. Thanks to ALL my parents, Barby Comins, Stuart Comins and Deborah Collier-Comins for their support and also for continuously "trying" when life brings them together. Thanks to K. Paige Engle, my book coach, for keeping me on schedule, to my Polka Dot Powerhouse sisters, and the neighborhood gang, for being my people.

ABOUT THE AUTHOR

Jody Comins, MSW is a Divorce & Family Mediator and Collaborative Coach in the Greater Boston area. She is an adult child of divorce and uses her experience to create a child-centered practice at A Better Way: Divorce Mediation, LLC. Jody is a court-approved facilitator for the required parenting classes in MA and teaches for The Divorce Center. She has been a mentor for volunteer mediators in the Norfolk Probate & Family Court.

Jody is the creator of *"Honor thy Children; Jewish Parenting through a Divorced Lens,"* which she presented with Rabbi Daniel Liben at the Association of Family and Conciliation Courts (AFCC) conference in Boston in 2017. Her blog series on "Speaking Out; Voices of Adult Children of Divorce" can be found on her website: http://www.divorcemediationabetterway.com

Jody earned a Master's of Social Work from Boston University and is both a founder of MetroWest Jewish Day School (MWJDS) in Framingham and a founding board member. She opened a local chapter of Polka Dot Powerhouse, a global women's connection group, in 2017. The chapter has grown to more than 150 members and offers women the opportunity to connect with other positive, like-minded women, personally and professionally, through monthly meetings, book clubs, conferences, and social events. Jody enjoys public speaking and has shared her messages of *"How to Get out of Your Own Way; Setting and Keeping Intentions"* and *"Effective Communication; How to Listen and Be Heard in Everyday Conversation"* around the country in local workshops & conferences. You can contact her at jodycomins@me.com to arrange a speaking engagement.

Jody has lived in Framingham, MA since 1997 with her husband, Mike Schnur, and daughters Talia (a rising junior at the University of Miami) and Elizabeth (a rising senior at Gann Academy in Waltham, MA).